Marie-Claire Di Carlo

Take This Course Before You Divorce

Marie-Claire Di Carlo

Take This Course Before You Divorce

for Love beyond the Grave

Blessed Hope Publishing

Imprint
Any brand names and product names mentioned in this book are subject to trademark, brand or patent protection and are trademarks or registered trademarks of their respective holders. The use of brand names, product names, common names, trade names, product descriptions etc. even without a particular marking in this work is in no way to be construed to mean that such names may be regarded as unrestricted in respect of trademark and brand protection legislation and could thus be used by anyone.

Cover image: www.ingimage.com

Publisher:
Blessed Hope Publishing
is a trademark of
International Book Market Service Ltd., member of OmniScriptum Publishing Group
17 Meldrum Street, Beau Bassin 71504, Mauritius

Printed at: see last page
ISBN: 978-613-7-88672-4

Love is patient , Love is kind…

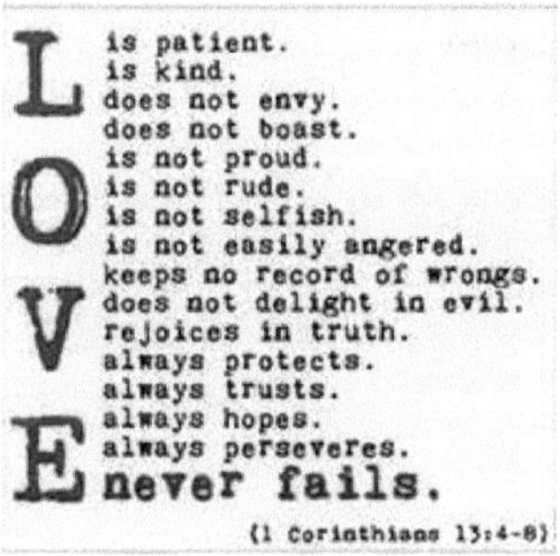

Here are 11 exercises to do emotionally that can hopefully help your situation I you are heading for a divorce. This mini course you can do together or apart. I wish you the best of luck and hope that your love rekindles and that you both are happier than you've ever been.

1.Believe that your love was divinely united.

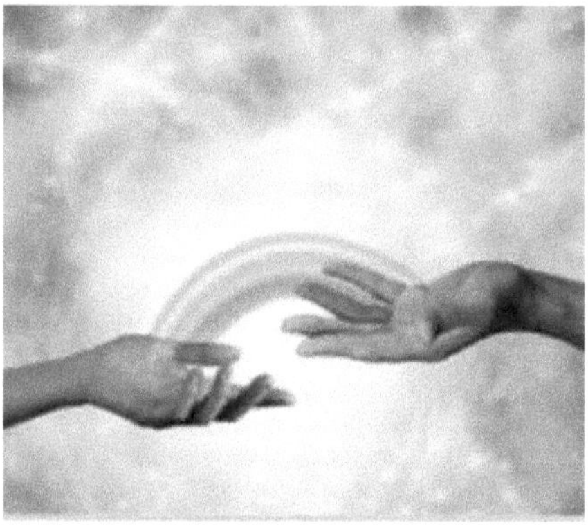

I'm not a match maker and am not going to easily put you too back together. You will do that. I'm just guiding you the right direction. I believe that every couple has a sacredness to them that the divine implanted in them. And I also believe that angels guided you too together. Believing also will keep you united during the hard times, during the rough fights and will bring you with faith and hope to stay together. Love is a divine gift from God for two people to share.

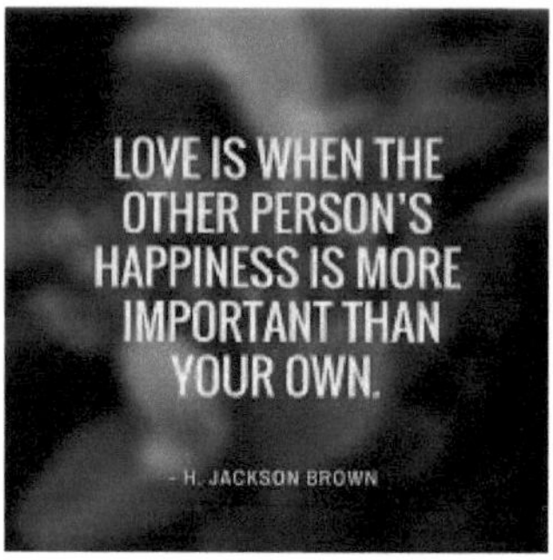
LOVE IS WHEN THE
OTHER PERSON'S
HAPPINESS IS MORE
IMPORTANT THAN
YOUR OWN.
- H. JACKSON BROWN

2. List all the good qualities of your partner. Compliment them.

Positive Character Traits

kind
generous
enthusiastic
responsible
brave
honest
hard working
imaginitive
intelligent
trustworthy
optimistic
unselfish
considerate
helpful
encouraging
polite
careful
ambitious
modest
reliable
clever

reliable
energetic
upbeat
understanding
confident
observant
compassionate
insightful
witty
flexible
supportive
organized
determined
humorous
respectful
caring
empathetic
forgiving
persistent
sincere
accepting

easygoing
creative
considerate
thoughtful
artistic
cooperative
cheerful
motivated
courageous
open-minded
patient
reasonable
outgoing
independent
articulate
dedicated
focused
generous
quiet
thorough
positive

I know right now you might be upset but put those feelings aside and do this love exercise. What do you love about you partner? Make the list as long or short as you like. Then show your partner. You can both do the exercise if you like.

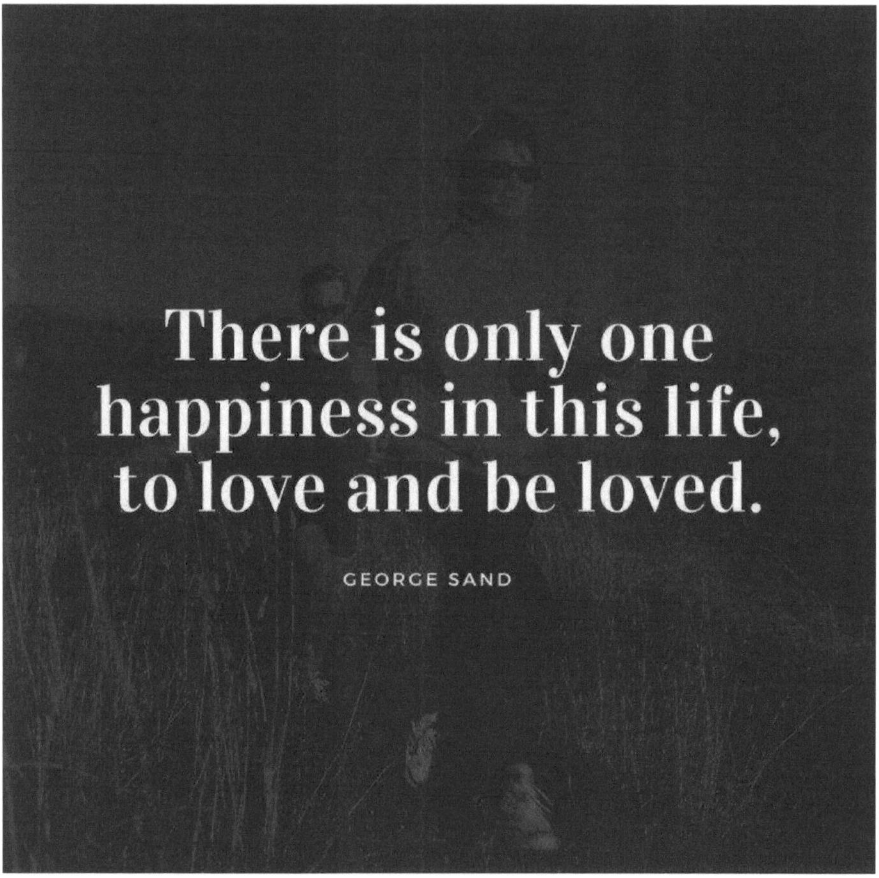
There is only one happiness in this life, to love and be loved.
GEORGE SAND

3. Remember a great memory that the two of you share.

MEMORY IMPROVEMENT

Now is the time to practice your memory. Remember the time you fell in love and how that felt, and how they made you feel. Fall in love all over again. Maybe the person has changed a little or a lot, that's ok so have you. Time changes you together and as long as you remember that you once loved, you'll always fall in love again and again. The memory is too strong, but you have to remember.

The happiest couples never have the same character. They have the best understanding of their differences.

4. Remember a great love making session.

You can't get more sacred then lovemaking. That's where all the magic is. It's where your child or children were born is you have any. If you don't there's still magic there. Sometimes it's the best memories we have of our partner. Remember how hot your partner got you and why you love them so much.

THE BEST RELATIONSHIP
IS WHEN YOU
CAN ACT LIKE LOVERS
AND BEST FRIENDS AT
THE SAME TIME.

5. What qualities do your kids have of your partner.

Like father, like son.
VectorStock

This exercise is for those with kids obviously. No one reminds you more of your partner than your kid or kids. They have their eyes, or they have your attitude. They are the fruit of love. If your kid or kids are adopted they naturally pick up on our gestures and expressions. Name the qualities that your kids have from their mom or dad.

Love begins by
smiling together.
Love lasts by
laughing together.

6. Remember when you first met.

The Day We First Met
by
sparkle_princess15

Nothing is more magical than the day you first met. Just these flashbacks can make you reconsider divorce. It was a destined meet. The angels were there pushing you too together. Now its up to you to let the story continue.

"My life has been such a wonderful adventure since you came along."
UPJOURNEY

7. What does your partner do that turns you on?

Turn Me On
3D ASMR

Our most intimate moments together reveal their secrets. We know how much they like this and how much we like that. Cherish those moments of pleasure, remember them. Three of four times what brings a couple back together is the love making.

"Forget the fairy tales, I think our love story is the best one ever told."
UPJOURNEY

8. Remember when your child or children were born.

Another magical moment is when your kid or kids were born. Again, this one only applies to those with kids. The fruit of your love. There's a mystery about childbirth. It takes a man and a woman and God to conceive a child. That child will grow up to be their own individual but with both your characteristics. The magic of love.

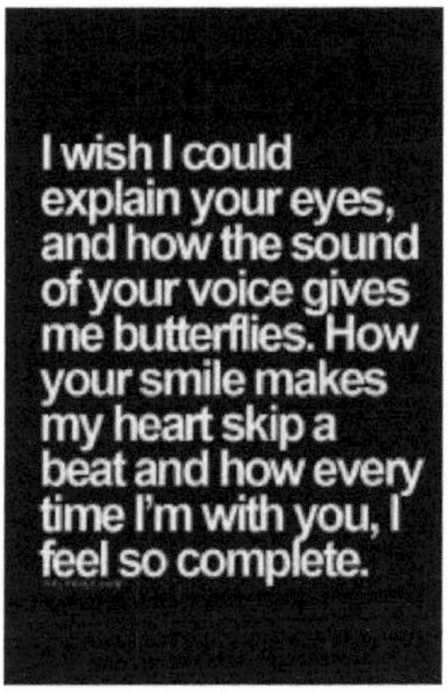
I wish I could explain your eyes, and how the sound of your voice gives me butterflies. How your smile makes my heart skip a beat and how every time I'm with you, I feel so complete.

9. Give a gift from the heart to your partner.

You are a gift

No one knows our partner like we do. What music they like, their hobbies, and so forth. It doesn't have to be Christmas to give your partner a gift from the heart to show them that they care. This exercise would be fun to do the both of you. You'd be surprised how well your partner knows you.

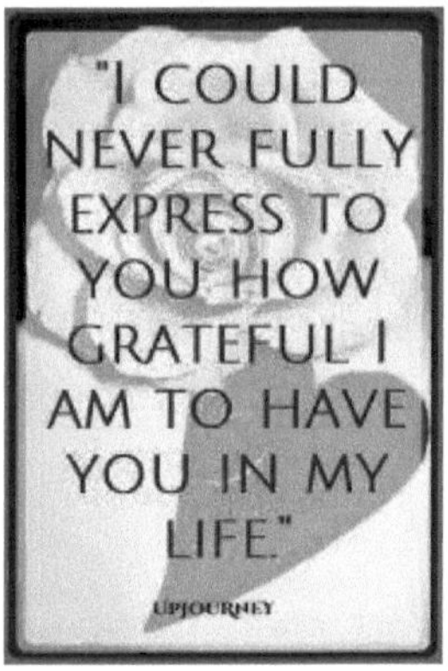
"I COULD NEVER FULLY EXPRESS TO YOU HOW GRATEFUL I AM TO HAVE YOU IN MY LIFE."
UPJOURNEY

10. Imagine if you weren't fighting what you would be doing.

Fighting is for misunderstandings. When a couple understands each other they don't need to fight all the time. Think about it. If you weren't fighting what fun would you be doing together? What fun are you missing out on? Traveling together, loving making, sight-seeing, going to the beach and so forth, you fill in the blanks. Fight for each other not at each other.

BEHIND EVERY HAPPY COUPLE LIES TWO PEOPLE WHO HAVE FOUGHT HARD TO OVERCOME ALL OBSTACLES AND INTERFERENCE TO BE THAT WAY.
WHY? BECAUSE IT'S WHAT THEY WANTED.
ilovemylsi.com

11. Forgive.

God's
gift of love allows you to
experience true
FORGIVENESS

Last but not least forgive. God's love is divine and He wants us to love each other profoundly like He does. His love forgives all our shortcomings. So why can't we forgive our partners'? Forgiveness is divine. Be the bigger person and if it's you that needs forgiveness, pray and pray a lot that you are forgiven. I hope this book helps you get back on track on your love story. Peace and lots of love xoxox.

MIX
Papier aus verantwortungsvollen Quellen
Paper from responsible sources
FSC® C105338

Printed by Books on Demand GmbH, Norderstedt / Germany